Richland County Public Library
1431 Assembly Street Columbia .SC .29201
www.richland.lib.sc.us

D1468536

Famous Explorers

Hernando de Soto

Tanya Larkin

The Rosen Publishing Group's
PowerKids Press™
New York

For Antoine

Published in 2001 by The Rosen Publishing Group, Inc.
29 East 21st Street, New York, NY 10010

Copyright © 2001 by The Rosen Publishing Group, Inc.

All rights reserved. No part of this book may be reproduced in any form without permission in writing from the publisher, except by a reviewer.

Photo Credits: Cover and title page, pp. 2, 3, 9, 16 © Granger Collection; pp. 4, 8, 11, 12, 19 © North Wind Pictures; pp. 7, 13, 15 © Corbis-Bettmann; pp. 2, 3, 20 © SuperStock; p. 23 © Tate Gallery, London/Art Resource, NY.

First Edition

Book Design: Maria E. Melendez and Felicity Erwin

Larkin, Tanya.
      Hernando de Soto / by Tanya Larkin.
        p. cm.— (Famous explorers)
      Includes index.
      Summary: A biography of the wealthy Spanish explorer who became the first white man to cross the Mississippi.
      ISBN 0-8239-5557-5 (lib. bdg. : alk. paper)
      1.Soto, Hernando de, ca. 1500–1542—Juvenile literature. 2. Explorers—America—Biography—Juvenile literature. 3. Explorers—Spain—Biography—Juvenile literature. 4. Southern states—Discovery and exploration—Spanish—Juvenile literature. [1.De Soto, Hernando, ca. 1500–1542. 2. Explorers.] I. Title. II. Series.

E125.S7 L37 2000
970.01′6′092—dc21
[B]   99-056151

Manufactured in the United States of America

Contents

4

A Dream of His Own

Hernando de Soto was born in Spain in the early 1500s. As a young boy, he saw sailors returning from a faraway place called the Indies. The sailors brought home gold and other goods. They also told stories about their adventures. De Soto decided that he wanted to have adventures, too. His parents wanted him to stay in Spain and become a lawyer. De Soto did not like that idea.

De Soto went on his first adventure, called an **expedition**, when he was still a teenager. He and some other men went to Panama, in Central America. They were looking for gold and new land for a Spanish **colony**. On the expedition to Panama, de Soto showed that he was a smart and brave leader.

Hernando de Soto led Spanish expeditions in North and South America.

Victory on Horseback

In 1532, de Soto joined Pizarro, another Spanish explorer, on an expedition for gold in Peru. Peru is on the west coast of South America. In order to get the gold, the soldiers understood that they would have to **conquer** the Inca Indians who lived in Peru.

Pizarro made de Soto captain of the **cavalry**. He ordered de Soto to **capture** Cajamarca. That was where the Inca emperor, Atahuallpa, lived. The Spaniards knew that they could conquer the Inca people with their horses. De Soto and his men rode their horses straight at the Incas. The Incas did not fight back. They had never seen horses before. They thought that the Spaniards were gods because they had animals with silver feet. The "feet of silver" were just iron **horseshoes**.

Pizarro led horses through the mountains of South America. →

The Incas

The Incas had a rich **civilization**. In some cities they put down streets. They built beautiful buildings along these streets in a pattern that looked like the sun and its rays. The Incas made **ceremonial** costumes out of gold, silver, and bird feathers. They invented new ways to water their crops. They also discovered plants that helped heal sick people.

The Spaniards were not interested in the Incas. They just wanted gold. The Spaniards killed almost all of the Incas in battle and destroyed their cities. Without guns or horses, the Incas could not defend themselves. The Incas who survived the battles were killed by diseases brought over by the Europeans.

An Inca silver container in the shape of a musician (above).
The inside of the Incas' temple of the Sun (left).

The Bored Conqueror

De Soto was a very rich **conquistador** when he returned to Spain. He lived a comfortable life in Spain. He married a **noblewoman** and they lived in a fancy house in the city of Seville. They had many servants.

Family life soon became boring for the conquistador. De Soto needed a challenge. He no longer wanted to work for Pizarro's army. He wanted to be the **governor** of his own colony. He asked King Charles I of Spain if he could conquer more lands in the Americas. King Charles I gave de Soto permission to conquer the part of North America that we now call Florida. King Charles I also made de Soto the governor of Cuba, an island not far from Florida.

De Soto needed new challenges to be happy. →

11

De Soto's Florida

D e Soto left Spain in April 1538 with about 700 people. His **fleet** was made up of 10 large ships. Twenty smaller ships traveled with them. The ships protected each other against pirates. It took de Soto and his fleet nearly two months to sail across the Atlantic Ocean to the island of Cuba.

De Soto and his soldiers spent a year in Cuba fixing ships and buying supplies for their trip to the North American **mainland**. When they finally left Cuba, they sailed for about one week before reaching shore. The expedition landed in what is now called Tampa Bay. De Soto and his men continued north. They spent the winter in a small Indian village.

Explorers' maps of Florida were not completely correct (above). De Soto and his men were excited to finally reach Florida (left).

War in the Swamps

De Soto could never have prepared for what he found in Florida. He thought he could conquer anyone because he had conquered the Incas in South America. The Timucuan Indians of Florida were different than the Incas, though. The Timucuans had met unfriendly Spanish people before. They did not trust the Spaniards as the Incas had at first.

The Timucuans hid in the **swamps** and shot arrows at de Soto and his army. De Soto's men were not used to war in the swamps. The soldiers' feet sank in the mud. The soldiers could not fire their guns as often as the Indians could shoot their arrows. Many soldiers complained about being hungry and hot. Some even went back to Cuba.

The Spaniards fought on horses and used swords and armor. The Indians used clubs and bows and arrows in battle.

The Path to Gold

De Soto figured out a way to fight the Timucuan Indians. He captured the chief of each Timucuan village. This scared the other Indians. The Indians **surrendered** to de Soto. They were afraid that de Soto might kill both them and their leaders.

The Spanish soldiers still didn't know how to **survive** in the swamps. They were starving by the time they reached an Indian village. They gathered corn and cabbage on the way, but they had a hard time hunting for meat. The Spaniards stole the Indians' food. De Soto asked each village chief where he could find gold. He got angry when the chiefs told him that there was no gold around. He was sure that the chiefs were lying to him.

The Spanish soldiers had a hard time getting food. Like the Indians, they gathered corn to eat.

The Indians Fight Back

De Soto heard that there was a lot of grain in a place called Cale. He also heard that soldiers there had helmets made of gold. When De Soto and his men arrived, they did not find any gold. De Soto was angry. He thought that if he returned to Spain without gold, he would lose his power.

De Soto took his anger out on the Indians. He kidnapped them and made them **slaves**. The news of de Soto's cruelty reached other Indian villages in Florida. The Indians tried to protect themselves. When the Spaniards arrived in Napituca, the Indian chief Vitachuco invited de Soto to a **feast**. The chief planned a surprise attack on the Spaniards. De Soto found out about the attack. He attacked the Indians first and won the battle.

The Spaniards captured the Indians and made them work as slaves.

The Mississippi River

De Soto traveled north through Florida to what is now the state of Georgia. In the village of Cofitachequi, de Soto met a kind female chief. He called her La Señora, which means "the lady" in Spanish. La Señora tried to please the Spaniards so that they would not hurt her and her people. She gave de Soto her own necklace of pearls. The soldiers wanted gold, not pearls. They kidnapped La Señora and used her as a guide. She later escaped.

De Soto decided to travel west. He fought more battles with Indians. In May of 1541, he came across a river. He named the river Rio Grande, which means "big river" in Spanish. It was later renamed the Mississippi River. De Soto was the first European to reach the Mississippi River.

De Soto reached the Mississippi River while traveling in what is now the state of Mississippi.

De Soto's Legacy

De Soto was the first Spanish explorer to travel far into the mainland of North America and to reach the great Mississippi River. For three years, he and his men explored the land. It was a hard journey. The Spaniards often fought with the Indians, and they never found the gold they wanted. In 1542, de Soto fell sick with a fever. He died on the banks of the Mississippi. Later, explorers set up colonies on the land de Soto had explored.

De Soto's Timeline

Early 1500s–De Soto is born in Spain.

1532–De Soto joins Pizarro's voyage to Peru.

1539–De Soto lands in Florida.

1541–De Soto reaches the Mississippi River.

1542–De Soto dies at the banks of the Mississippi.

Glossary

capture (KAP-chur) To take over land or take control of people.

cavalry (KAH-vul-ree) The part of an army that rides horses.

ceremonial (sehr-ih-MOH-nee-ul) Having to do with special occasions.

civilization (sih-vuh-lih-ZAY-shun) A group of people living in an organized and similar way.

colony (KAH-luh-nee) An area in a new country where a large group of people move. The people are still ruled by the leaders and laws of their old country.

conquer (KON-ker) To take control of people or land by using violence.

conquistador (kon-KEES-tuh-dor) A Spanish explorer who tries to take over land.

expedition (ek-spuh-DIH-shun) A trip for a special purpose.

feast (FEEST) A large meal.

fleet (FLEET) Many ships under the command of one person.

governor (GUH-vuh-nur) An official that is put in charge of a colony by a king or queen.

horseshoes (HORS-shooz) Bands of iron nailed to a horse's hooves to protect them.

mainland (MAYN-land) A large piece of land next to an ocean.

noblewoman (NOH-bul-wuh-man) A member of royalty or another high-ranking person of a kingdom.

slaves (SLAYVZ) People who were "owned" by another person and were forced to work for him or her.

surrendered (suh-REN-derd) To have given up.

survive (sur-VYV) To stay alive.

swamps (SWOHMPS) Wetlands with lots of trees and bushes.

Index

A
arrows, 14
Atahuallpa, 6

B
battles, 9, 18, 21

C
Charles I, King, 10
chiefs, 17, 18, 21
conquistador, 10

E
expedition, 5, 6, 13

G
gold, 5, 6, 9, 17, 18, 22

I
Inca Indians, 6, 9, 14

L
La Señora, 21

M
Mississippi River, 21, 22

P
pirates, 13
Pizarro, 6, 10

S
sailors, 5
slaves, 18
soldiers, 6, 13, 14, 17, 18
Spaniards, 6, 9, 14, 17, 18, 21

T
Timucuan Indians, 14, 17

V
Vitachuco, 18

Web Sites

To learn more about Hernando de Soto, check out these Web sites:

http://www.optonline.com/comptons/ceo/01267_A.html
http://www.cr.nps.gov/delta/desoto.htm

RICHLAND COUNTY PUBLIC LIBRARY

3 0080 02288 0609

JB   Soto
Larkin, Tanya
Hernando de Soto /

30080022880609 18.75   SA

RICHLAND COUNTY PUBLIC LIBRARY
COLUMBIA, SOUTH CAROLINA 29201

RCPL MAR 0 5 2002